Mary

Mysteries of the Blessed Virgin Mary

by Dr Francesca Murphy

All booklets are published thanks to the generous support of the members of the Catholic Truth Society

CATHOLIC TRUTH SOCIETY
PUBLISHERS TO THE HOLY SEE

Contents

The Practice of Marian Devotion

Devotion to the mother of Jesus Christ is a peculiar thing. An anthropologist of religion who wanted to study this phenomenon would encounter devout ladies chanting the rosary together before Mass on Saturday mornings. He would notice the whiff of corporate solidarity given off by a Catholic congregation when it sings a Marian hymn. Having detected that these are the only hymns which Catholics join in for, and loudly, he might feel as if he were watching someone else's football club celebrating a victory. Having fought his way through crowded streets to join the queue for the grotto in Lourdes, he would probably classify devotion to Mary as a type of corporate piety. He wouldn't be completely wrong, because Marian devotion does express the identity which all Catholics share. As the mother of the son of God, Mary is the mother of every person who becomes a son or daughter of God in baptism. Devotion to Mary does reflect our identity as members of the one Church. And yet, as the mother of the Lord, Mary is unique, the most singular woman who ever lived. So the devotion of Christians to Mary is always a personal thing.

Newcomers need help in entering the practice and the spirit of Marian devotion. But it may not help to suggest what emotions one ought to feel about Mary: Marian devotion engages every human heart in its own way. Like the anthropologist, the baptised Catholic can observe these collective devotions and fear that if someone took our notebook away and invited us to join in, we would have the wrong sort of emotions, or none at all. Telling someone else how to feel about Mary is like telling them how to love their own mother. It doesn't work. What *can* be helpful is to describe the practices which Catholics have used over the centuries and to explain how our love for Mary can bring us closer to Christ, her Son. If your response to Mary is unique to you, join the club!

The Rosary

The art of saying the rosary is to use the *words* of the prayers to concentrate one's mind on God, whilst *thinking* about the stages in the Gospel. These stages are the 'mysteries' of the Rosary. Each 'round' of five decades or 'mystery' is a portal into the life of Christ. When I was being received into the Church nearly 25 years ago, there were three acknowledged collections of meditations: the 'Glorious Mysteries,' the 'Joyful Mysteries,' and the 'Sorrowful Mysteries.' I followed a typical exchange in the letters column of a Catholic newspaper about whether it is OK to invent new mysteries, with the conservative rosary-sayers insisting that one must do as the Church has always done, and the progressivists insisting that their children enjoyed thinking up mysteries from the Biblical stories. Eventually, John Paul II outwitted both camps by defining on behalf of the Church a new spectrum for meditation: the 'Mysteries of Light.' Saying the rosary is travelling through the stages in the Incarnation, and remembering his life as a glorious event, as something joyful, as sorrowful, and as luminous.

The Mysteries

The Resurrection, the first 'Glorious mystery,' is followed by (2) the Ascension, (3) Pentecost, (4) the Assumption of Mary, and the Coronation of Mary as queen of heaven (5). These mysteries reveal the *glory* of God. They show us something of heaven. The 'Joyful Mysteries' are the happy events of (1) the Annunciation to Mary by the Angel Gabriel, (2) the Visitation of Mary to Elizabeth, (3) the birth of Jesus, (4) the presentation of Jesus in the Temple (when the old priest, Simeon, says, 'Let thy servant depart in peace, for I have seen thy salvation,' *Lk* 2.30), and (5) the 'finding' of Jesus, teaching the Scribes. I once said the Joyful Mysteries with a friend just before she went into hospital to have her second baby. My friend said that these mysteries correspond to the steps of having a baby: first you find out you are pregnant, you tell your friends the news, the baby is born, you have the baby baptised...and then the child grows up, and makes his way into the world. The 'Sorrowful Mysteries' recall that, on Good Friday, Christ became the man of sorrows. We pray and reflect on (1) Jesus' agony in the Garden, (2) his scourging at the pillar, (3) his crowning with thorns, (4) his carrying the Cross to Golgotha, and (5) his crucifixion and death. Probably, some people now picture scenes from Mel Gibson's *The Passion of the Christ* when they meditate on these mysteries, recreating the movie in their mind's eye.

Pictures have a way of sticking in one's mind, and visualisation can help us to reflect. When the rosary meditations were first set out in their modern form, in 1483, illustrated books, with wood-cuts of each of the mysteries, were printed for people to look at while they told their beads. John Paul II suggested that one can combine saying the rosary with various kinds of visual aids, like icons: "Announcing each mystery, and perhaps even using a suitable icon to portray it, is as it were to *open up a scenario* on which to focus our attention. The words direct the imagination and the mind towards a particular episode or moment in the life of Christ. In the Church's traditional spirituality, the veneration of icons and the many devotions appealing to the senses, ...make use of visual and imaginative elements (the *compositio loci*), judged to be of great help in concentrating the mind on a particular mystery. This is a methodology...which *corresponds to the inner logic of the Incarnation*: in Jesus, God wanted to take on human features. It is through his bodily reality that we are led into contact with the mystery of his divinity."[1]

Mysteries of Light

Down to 2002, Rosary devotion centred on the joyful beginning of the Incarnation, its sorrowful climax, and its glorious conclusion. But if the rosary is, as Pius XII said, "the compendium of the entire Gospel", what about the middle of the Gospel drama? In his 'Apostolic Letter on the Most Holy Rosary,' John Paul II proposed the 'Mysteries of Light,' in which Christ figures as the *teacher* of his disciples: (1) the Baptism by John in the Jordan, (2) the Wedding at Cana, (3) the Proclamation of the Kingdom of God, (4) Christ's Transfiguration and (5) his Institution of the Eucharist, at the last supper.

These mysteries are said on Thursdays. When the early Church Fathers talked about 'illumination,' they meant the reception of insight into God. 'Illumination' is a less prosaic way of saying 'education.' John Paul said that, in the luminous stages of his life, "Christ is the supreme Teacher, the revealer and the one revealed. ...Contemplating the scenes of the Rosary in union with Mary is a means of learning from her to 'read' Christ, to discover his secrets and to understand his message."[2]

You can see that the Rosary's four types of 'mystery' reflect certain kinds of human emotion, like joy and sorrow. But no one is obliged to *feel* depressed when they say the sorrowful mysteries, or illuminated on Thursdays and uplifted on Wednesdays and Sundays! The names for the mysteries reflect the character of the *events* on which we reflect when we pray the rosary. To say the rosary is to recall a sequence of real, historical events.

Repetitive Prayer

Praying on beads is an ancient custom, and a useful one, because otherwise one is liable to lose count. But of course you can say the rosary without the beads: for instance, if you work in an office, you can say a decade or so when you are doing some photocopying, using the 1-9 buttons as an abacus – just remember to throw in number 10! The ubiquity of cell phones has made it impossible for the casual observer to tell the difference between someone talking to a friend, someone silently whispering the rosary, and those eccentrics who talk to invisible friends. Praying the rosary is a bit of all three. It is a good habit, because it turns our thoughts away from ourselves, even at work, and toward the things that matter.

In the 11th century, lay Cistercian monks got the habit of combining humdrum work with repetitive prayer. Since they couldn't read, these monks were dispensed from going into Church to recite the psalms, and said 150 'Our Fathers' instead! 150 corresponded to the number of psalms in the psalter. Another prayer which became popular for repetitive use was the Angelic Salutation, the first half of our 'Hail Mary': *Ave Maria, gratia plena, Dominus tecum. Benedicta tu in mulieribus* ('Hail Mary, full of grace, the Lord is with you. Blessed art thou among women'). In the Christian Middle Ages, no one worried about offending people by using religious gear. So it was natural to carry quite large ropes of 150 beads, for chanting the 'Our Father' or, as was common by the 12th century, doing 150 Angelic Salutations, each followed by 'Jesus Christ. Amen'. Eventually, people looked for something more expansive than the Annunciation scene and the Holy

Name. So, in around 1409-1415, a Carthusian monk, Dominic of Prussia, set out no less than fifty key points of the life of Christ, on which to meditate whilst saying one's *Aves*. Two examples are #5: 'Jesus Christ whom thou didst wrap in swaddling clothes and laid in a manger. Amen' and #19: 'Jesus Christ whose feet Mary Magdalene washed with her tears and wiped with her hair, kissed and anointed. Amen.'[3]

Dominican origins of the Rosary

It was a Dominican friar who realised that, if the Ave was too little, fifty key stages in the Incarnation were too much for anyone to remember. In 1483, this practical friar published *Our Dear Lady's Psalter*, the illustrated rosary book mentioned above: it contains the three major stages (Glorious, Sorrowful and Joyful) with just 15 meditation points, all but one of which are the same as we say today. Apart from the accessible number of meditations, what may have fixed this particular set was the picture book. This combination of repetitive prayer with reflection on easily memorable scenes of the Incarnation caught on and entered the ordinary Catholic's prayer life. In 1520, Pope Leo X commended this practice. In the period of the English Reformation, owning sets of beads was a mark of one who adhered to the 'Old Faith.' By the time Pope Pius V formally approved the rosary devotion, in 1569, and the Council of Trent included in its Breviary, in 1570, the Rosary had taken the form it has today, with the full 'Hail Mary,' including the second half, 'pray for us sinners, now and at the hour of our death,' and the 'Our Father' commencing the decades and the 'Glory be' concluding them. Dominicans were active in promoting the rosary – it was another Dominican friar, Alberto da Castello who invented the term 'mystery' to describe the stages for contemplation. Some theologians, and some lay visionaries, have done their best to make 'Mariology' something exotic. The Fathers of the Second Vatican Council had a more everyday theology of Mary, defining the Mother of the Lord in terms of the key rosary meditations.[4]

Looked at from the outside in, the Rosary devotion sounds like a string of slurred prayers to 'Holy Mary, Mother of God'. Everyone who says it is on the 'outside' at some time, and not just anthropologists or casual onlookers, but, for instance, children who are compelled to do it by devout grown-ups, and adult converts who try to develop the practice without any parallel experience of saying one set of words whilst thinking about 'something else.' Learning to say the rosary is like learning any skill; it takes time to do it thoughtfully, and from the inside. The difficult part of the learning curve can be *combining* the mechanics of it – the words – with the meditation. Why say the 'Hail Mary' whilst thinking about the Ascension or the Transfiguration? When he announced his Marian encyclical, *Redemptoris Mater* (*The Mother of the Redeemer*) on the Feast of Mary, Mother of God, 1st January, 1987, Pope John Paul II described Mary as the "memory of the Church." The Bible contains the written record of the historical life of Christ and of the primitive Church. Mary is the living record of these events, the woman who personally recollects them. It can help us climb the learning curve of combining 'rote words' with Incarnation meditations if we consider that Mary remembers the historical events alongside us, and with us, as we pray. One modern theologian comments that, "Again and again in recent Marian apparitions the Rosary has played a part: ...Mary has fingered the beads along with those praying the Rosary. Why should this be? ...so that it is from her point of view, from her memory that we should look at the mysteries of Jesus' life... We are forgetful. Things we have already heard too often fade in our memory. But Mary's memory is throughout all these thousands of years as fresh as on the first day."[5]

Apparitions, Hymns and Feasts

Some Modern Apparitions – and Shrines

What the Catholic Church calls "public revelation" from God came to an end with the death of the last Apostle. With the death of the 'last Apostle,' sacred Scripture was complete and could never be added to. The Church also acknowledges that some "private revelations" have occurred, which add nothing new to the faith deposited in Scripture, but which remind us of that same faith. Appearances of Mary which the Church recognizes are thus "private revelations," not meant to displace the miracles in the Biblical salvation history, but to help us remember that miracles, or revelations from God, are at the heart of Christianity. Marian apparitions are part of the "private" rather than the public faith of the Church, a witness given to single individuals that God is with us.

A *Rolling Stone* journalist named Randall Sullivan wrote a book about a handful of recent Marian apparitions, from Medjugorje to a West Oregon trailer park. Investigating what he came to believe were miracles brought this anthropologist to the verge of Catholic faith. But in fact, none of the apparitions described in his book, *The Miracle Detective*, has yet been formally accepted by the Church. Of the nearly 400 appearances of Mary which people have staked a claim for in the 20th century, only eight have been officially recognized as "private revelation." When the Church acknowledges an apparition of Mary, it is giving building permission! Formal acceptance of a 'private revelation' enables the locals to set up a shrine or some other token of devotion to Mary on the site of the apparition. The eight holy places, or shrines which emerged in the last century as the result of an acknowledged apparition are Fatima, in Portugal, two in Belgium, Beauraing and Banneux, one in Japan, Akita, Syracuse in Italy, one in Manila, in Zeitoun in Egypt, and one in South America, Betania, in Venezuela. Because every shrine has its own typical statue, icon, or picture (like the image of our Lady of Guadalupe), the most well known 'face' of Mary in every country reflects the statues made for the shrines. The three famous 19th century Marian apparitions happened in France: to Catherine Labouré, in 1830, which gave rise to the 'Miraculous Medal' image of Mary, to Melane Calvat at La Salette in 1846, and that to Bernadette Subirous, at Lourdes in 1858.

Lourdes

I didn't intend to go to Lourdes. I missed the Dominican pilgrimage there because I was busy buying a house (*Lk* 14:18-20), and planned to make a trip to Tarascon instead, a few weeks later. For, earlier that summer, I'd read in *Le Monde* that a *"grotte"*, or cave was opening up in Tarascon for just two months. The *'grotte'* described by *Le Monde* shows the markings of human habitation from tens of thousands of years ago, with pictures on the walls of prehistoric animals. The most famous paleolithic cave paintings are those in Lascaux. Paleolithic art mostly depicts animals and fat ladies. Some archaeologists think the buxom paleolithic ladies are fertility symbols. The fact that our ancient ancestors didn't occupy all of their waking hours with making tools and hunting to eat is interesting. From the very beginning of human time, people have wanted to do more than just what it takes to survive. They have decorated their surroundings with beautiful artefacts. This human need to express itself in art is a sign that the human person is not just an evolutionary go-getter, but also a spirit, seeking to transcend its material conditions.

But, somehow, I ended up at Lourdes, watching those long queues of people feel the walls of a quite different *'grotte.'* It's well known that hundreds of people have claimed to recover from illnesses after a dip in the water from the Lourdes springs, and equally well known, to Catholic intellectuals, that the novelist Flannery O'Connor, suffering from the Lupus which eventually killed her, remarked on being compelled by her family to go to Lourdes, 'I'd rather die for my faith than take a bath for it.' Artistic people, who would love the caves at Tarascon and Lascaux, don't find Lourdes appealing. Some are depressed by the merchandising of Lourdes, the scores of shops selling cuckoo clocks, statuettes of the apparition, and plastic bottles for the holy water. But the main problem is that the heavy 19th century Church, and its grotto, are not really beautiful.

The difference between the lyrical images made by prehistoric artists and the images generated by the Marian apparitions is an important one. Although even the acknowledged apparitions are only deemed to be 'private revelations,' they give a key to the divine, public revelations recorded in Scripture which are the basis of Catholic faith. Paleolithic art expresses the spiritual side of early man, reaching out for the spiritual. The sites of the apparitions remind us of the divine reaching out for the human. If Mary really appeared at Lourdes, at Guadalupe, or at Manila in the Philippines, she was sent there by God. The Marian apparitions, and their shrines, are not about the human spirit stretching out for the divine, but about God using his Handmaid to reach out to human kind. When he was just a Cardinal, Joseph Ratzinger put it like this: "Mary is not ensconced merely in the past or merely in heaven, God's preserve. She is, and remains, present and active in this hour of history. She is an acting person here and today. Her life is not only behind us, and nor is it only above us. She goes before us... She interprets the historical moment for us, not through theories, but through action, through the action of showing us the way forward. ...in this texture of action it also comes to light who she is, who we *are*. But this happens only insofar as we become involved in the dynamic thrust of her figure."[6] The quaint images of the Marian shrines may not be appealing, to artistic sorts, but they can be literally touching, in that Mary, and so God, can touch our minds and bodies through them.

Marian Hymns

Catholics sing Marian anthems on the great Marian feast days, and at many other times. A new Catholic can feel quite awkward singing these emotional hymns, unless they are football fans and have got the hang of chorusing. The film *Educating Rita* has an old fashioned pub-singing scene - but that died out even before the smoking ban. People sing along at pop concerts, but they're really there for the guitar heroes in the bands. Then there's the last night of the Proms – and that's about it, for modern people. Still, we enjoy singing, for the same reasons people liked painting their caves – it's a way of wearing one's heart on one's sleeve. It's just that we've become unaccustomed to showing our souls in public.

The Salve Regina

One may feel out of place singing hymns to *Mary* because one has the ingrained belief that Church hymns ought to celebrate *God* or Christ, not any human being. This opinion became widespread in the 1970s, and many of the popular Marian anthems dropped out. Instead of singing to Mary after communion, we often sang hymns about what we mean to do for God, like *All that I am*. The result was not what it was intended to be, since these hymns often celebrate the *human communion* of the Church – instead of God! Professor Eamon Duffy described the attitude in some 1970s time-warp Catholic churches after the distribution of the Eucharist as "a comfortable sense of the simple continuum between human and divine community. The painful and contradictory sense of our unity in Christ despite our class and racial antagonisms…, the sheer brokenness of human society, is buried under a cosier sense of the niceness of all being together."[7] The Dominican chaplain in our Catholic Chaplaincy at Aberdeen University has enabled us to recover the right atmosphere for the post-communion moments of Mass by making the service conclude with the ancient Marian hymn, *Salve Regina*:

Salve Regina, Mater misericordiae,
Vita dulcedo et spes nostra salve.
Ad te clamamus exsules filii Hevae.
Ad te suspiramus gementes et flentes,
in hac lacrimarum valle.

Eja ergo advocata nostra, illos tuos misericordes oculos ad nos converte.
Et Jesum benedictum fructum ventris tui nobis post hoc exsilium ostende.
O clemens, o pia, o dulcis Virgo Maria.

Hail holy queen, mother of mercy,
Hail our life, our sweetness and our hope.
To you do we cry poor banished children of Eve,
To you do we send up our sighs, mourning and weeping in this vale of tears.

Turn then, most gracious advocate your eyes of mercy toward us.
And after this, our exile, Show us the fruit of your womb, Jesus.
O clement, O loving, O sweet Virgin Mary.

We sing it in Latin, and can veritably be said to belt it out. It works for three reasons. Like the 'cosy' 1970s folk hymns, the *Salve Regina* is also about the Church; but it is about the immaculate and perfect Church above and beyond our ordinary 'broken' lives. As the Queen of heaven, Mary represents the Church perfected by Christ: she already is what the Church as a whole will become at the end of history. In looking to her, we look to the authentic Church. It is into the hands of this perfect, feminine Church that Christ gave the power to make the Eucharist. Secondly, and I am no traditionalist or Tridentine rite advocate, it works because of the Latin: 'dulcis' is sweeter to sing than 'sweet', 'fructum ventris tui' tighter than 'fruit of thy womb.' The *Salve Regina* is good for corporate singing because it is slightly lugubrious, sad without tipping over into sentimentality. Like many great songs, it speaks of a profound yearning for that place which is over the rainbow. This ancient Marian anthem reminds us that 'over the rainbow' is not a sweet, hopeless hope, but a physical reality, a mother with her child. Like the 'Hail Mary', the *Salve Regina* nails the meaning of the Incarnation of God in human form in four little words: 'benedictum fructum ventris tui', 'the blessed fruit of your womb.' "A Catholic," Christopher Derrick once remarked, "cannot say the Hail Mary without mentioning the female generative tract."[8]

The Hail Holy Queen

I once spent a day working as a temp in a hospice. Or rather, half a day, and since temporary secretaries get paid by the hour, no notice was given of the brevity of the employment, and the text I typed smacked more of Christian Science than Incarnational Christianity, I had little cause to regard the place as a Christian hospital. After lunch, I went to the hospice Mass. A dozen or so haggard persons had collected there, some in their wheelchairs, and most barely able to stand. We concluded the Mass by singing the anthem which begins 'Hail, Queen of Heaven':

… the ocean star,
Guide of the wanderer here below;
Thrown on life's surge we claim thy care.
Save us from peril and from woe.
Mother of Christ, star of the sea,
Pray for the wanderer, pray for me.

And while to him who reigns above,
In godhead one, in persons three,
The source of life, of grace, of love,
Homage we pay on bended knee.
Virgin most pure, star of the sea,
Pray for the sinner, pray for me.

The only meaning and purpose of that hospice was in that Mass and in this hymn. Real Catholics don't shy away from vulnerability and mental and *physical* pain. Those who learn this hymn know instinctively that the Mother of Christ is the most real of Catholics, and feel they can confide the pain they feel in their bodies, as well as their souls, to her. Bad and lapsed Catholics may know this especially well: Bruce Springsteen makes his 9/11 fireman "see Mary in the garden" at the moment of his heroic death.[9]

The Church is an 'ark of salvation,' like Noah's ark. Following the Church Fathers, the Dominican mystic, Johann Tauler (1300-1361) understood Proverbs 31:10-31, which likens the "valiant woman" to a "merchant's ship", to refer to the Mother of all Christians. Tauler considered Mary as the 'ship' in whom all Christians sail. He based a devotional poem on this conceit:

A little ship is sailing
The silent waves between,
The richest gift she brings us,
Of all the world the Queen.

The sweetest gift she brings us
In silence sailing past,
Her mainsail is a love-song,
The Holy Ghost her mast.[10]

All the Marian hymns are love songs. This is why they look sappy to casual observers. Our love for our mother is not based in an emotion, but in a fact: she gave birth to us and natured us. No Christian faith is motherless, like Frankenstein. Mary, the mother of believers, helps our faith to come to life.

Marian Feasts

The liturgical calendar is marked with Marian feast days. Immediately after Christmas, on 1 January, comes the Solemnity of Mary. February has two, the Presentation of the Lord (in the temple, same as the fifth Joyful mystery) on the 2nd, and Our Lady of Lourdes, on the 11th. March sees the Feast of the Annunciation, on the 25th. May is dedicated to Mary, reflecting her youthful and springlike character. Gerard Manley Hopkins wrote a beautiful poem, "May Magnificat," about May as the month of Mary which you might want to look up, if you like poetry. June has Our Mother of Perpetual Help, on the 27th. The central Marian feast day in modern times is the Assumption. Celebrated on the 15th of August, this feast is a liturgical expression of the ancient dogma of the assumption of Mary into heaven. Belief that Mary was bodily assumed into heaven goes back to the 3rd or 4th century: it was sufficiently common place to form part of the 'Glorious Mysteries,' which, as we saw, were developed in the 15th century. There are Baroque paintings of Mary floating into heaven, encircled by ecstatic angels. The Assumption was defined by Pius XII in 1950. September has three Marian feasts, the 'Birth of Mary' on the 8th, 'Our Lady of Sorrows' on the 15th and a reminder of the mediaeval apparition of Mary in the Norfolk village of Walsingham, 'Our Lady of Walsingham,' on the 24th. Since the Church defines it as Rosary month, October has 'Our Lady of the Rosary,' on the 7th. The 'Presentation of the Blessed Virgin Mary,' is on 21st November. Building up through Advent to Christmas, December is given two important Marian feasts, the Immaculate Conception, on the 8th, and Our Lady of Guadalupe on the 12th.

Why so many feasts?

Why are so many days in the liturgical calendar devoted to Mary? It is to keep our minds on the end of time, which often seems too far off to be at all exciting. In Jesus' own time, many people were wanting to know when God would return in glory to set up his Paradise, the kingdom of God. In his answers to their questions, Jesus often makes the End of time sound very near indeed. He was not mistaken about this, for the End of ordinary history, or the 'Eschaton' happened with his

Resurrection from the dead. 'Time' was never the same again: a new world had begun to be born. The eternal world of God's new Paradise has already entered history. One human being already lives amongst us as one who has regained the innocence of the paradise lost by Adam and Eve. That person is Mary. The liturgical Calendar is marked with her feast days to remind us that ordinary time is not just going on, and on, after Christ, but that the Eschaton has peeped into our history. As Hugo Rahner suggests, the "last day and final judgement have begun already." For the "final glory" into which Mary has entered "is a recognition of the final glory of the Church. This indeed sometimes seems very far away in a remotely future time, but then we are often too shortsighted, and need to look close at hand, where we can find the heavenly reality hidden in our everyday lives."[11]

The Theology of Marian Devotion

The Two Sides of Mariology

The theology of Mary has two sides to it. One side connects up with Christ, with the Incarnation, and the other side is linked to the Church. The first formal doctrines taught by the Church about Mary were related to Christ (or 'Christological'). In the fifth century, disputes arose amongst theologians about the bond between Christ's human nature and his deity. Surely his divine nature could not be so closely bound up with his humanity that it went through the physical process of birth, and crawled around the floor in nappies? In order to keep Christ's divinity out of physical processes which revolt intellectuals, theologians were dreaming up clever ways of keeping it separate from his humanity. Others realised that the salvific effect of the Incarnation depends precisely on the divine nature of the Son becoming wholly and entirely bound up with the humanity of Jesus. To compartmentalise the divinity and humanity of Jesus in such a way that Mary is only the mother of the *man*, not of the Son of God, is to deny that the Word *really* became flesh (*Jn* 1:14). In order to safeguard the full reality of the Incarnation of God in the man Jesus Christ, the Ecumenical Councils of Ephesus (431) and Chalcedon (451) named Mary as '*Theo-tokos*', the God-bearer, meaning that she bore God within her womb.

Mary and the Incarnation

It may seem odd to us that Mary should have to be formally and dogmatically *defined* as the Mother of God. But historically, nearly every attempt to diminish the complete interpenetration of humanity *and divinity* in Christ has wanted to wriggle out of thinking of God himself as subject to the indignity of being carried about in the womb of a woman, and physically born. Marian devotion reinforces our sense of the concrete reality of the Incarnation of God. That was the purpose of the first formal, theological Mariology, as laid out in the title '*Theotokos*', given to Mary at Ephesus and Chalcedon. Putting Mary in the foreground backs up our belief that Jesus is not simply a highly inspired man, a spiritual genius, or someone to whom the spirit of God was always quite close, but, rather, God Himself in human *flesh*. It has wisely been said that, for the Word to be made flesh, it wasn't possible for Jesus to have a human father but no human *mother*: the basic presupposition of the incarnation is that a woman and mother should give birth to the Word. The way in to Mariology taken by most people, perhaps, and certainly the way in taken by the first dogmatic definitions, is Christological. The Incarnational side of Mariology highlights her *sacramental* significance, the way in which her *body* became the temple and dwelling place of God. In order to "dwell amongst us" (*Jn* 1:14), God had first to indwell the 'temple' of Mary's womb. All religions have sacred spaces and places, and, in her role as the bearer of the Lord, Mary is the supreme 'sacred place.'

Mary and the Church

When Christians think of sacred spaces, they are likely to think of church buildings. Many particular churches are connected by name or by dedication to Our Lady (the Cathedral in my hometown is dedicated to 'Our Lady of Aberdeen,' for instance). This helps to concretise her link to ecclesiology, the science of the Church. Even before the title of "God-bearer" was formally given to Mary, theologians had had much to say about her. The claims which the early Church and Patristic theologians made about her were tied to their idea of the Church. They spoke of Mary as the *mother* of all believers, generating, giving birth to and nourishing Christians, just as the Church does. As the 'archetype' of the Church, Mary is someone different from Christ, just as every human member of the Church is someone different from Christ. The second side of Mariology, which is ecclesiological, highlights the reality of Mary, and thus of all Christians, as persons who co-operate with Christ. In terms of Church dogma, this side of Mariology has been emphasized since the Protestant Reformation, and it is probably the main reason why some Protestants think that Mariolatry (or inappropriate devotion to Mary) and Mariology are one and the same thing. Because the 16th century Protestant Reformers seemed to think of God's grace and human action as a zero-sum game, in which the human is entirely out numbered by the divine, the Catholics, in turn, emphasised that human beings co-operate with God's grace. The word 'co-operation' is important here: it takes *two*, God and a created person, to *co*-operate. Mary has always been in the frontline of this debate, as the most outstanding example of the co-operation of divine and human action which Catholic doctrine attests. For Catholics, Mary is the living token of the fact that divine grace acts through created persons, not replacing them or making them God's ventriloquists or puppets on a divine string. "Mariology," Ratzinger says, "demonstrates that the doctrine of grace does not revoke creation, but is the definitive Yes to creation."[12]

Free co-operation with God

Divinity and humanity come together in Christ's incarnation, and grace and nature interpenetrate in every baptised person, working together, not against each other, because nature is God's creation. *Lumen Gentium* summed up the Catholic teaching when it stated that "the holy Fathers," the Patristic and mediaeval doctors of the Church "see her as used by God not merely in a passive way, but as freely cooperating in the work of human salvation through faith and obedience. For, as St. Irenaeus says, she 'being obedient, became the cause of salvation for herself and for the whole human race.'"[13] Mary and indeed all graced believers are real *actors* or agents within God's plan. Catholics think of Mary or the Church, and Christ, as having a symbiotic unity, like husband and wife do, but also as being different from one another, as husband and wife are. Two of the most famous Marian dogmas of the past two centuries, the Immaculate Conception (1854) and the Assumption (1950) are directed to Mary as someone who is a person in her own right.

The 'Incarnational' and 'Ecclesial' sides of Mariology are different without, of course, being absolutely distinct. The Vatican II Constitution *Lumen Gentium* describes Mary's 'cooperation' with Christ's grace as being a consequence of her physical "conception" of Christ and maternal companionship with him in his earthly ministry. *Lumen Gentium* says that Mary "is hailed as a pre-eminent and singular member of the Church, and as its type and excellent exemplar in faith and charity. The Catholic Church, taught by the Holy Spirit, honors her with filial affection and piety as a most beloved mother...the Blessed Virgin was in this earth the virgin Mother of the Redeemer... She conceived, brought forth and nourished Christ. She presented Him to the Father in the temple, and was united with Him by compassion as He died on the Cross. In this singular way she cooperated by her obedience, faith, hope and burning charity in the work of the Saviour in giving back supernatural life to souls. Wherefore she is our mother in the order of grace."[14]

Mary 'type' of the Church

But how can Mary be an individual – the historical, Jewish woman about whom historians writes – *and* the whole Church – thousands and thousands of persons, throughout history? Isn't it just a sort of metaphor? Yes and no. It is certainly intended to be taken symbolically, or allegorically, rather than literally. Because they believed that God is the ultimate author of Scripture, the Fathers of the Church thought of everyone, and everything in Scripture as having some allegorical meaning. For instance, Augustine, and Irenaeus before him, thought of Noah's Ark as an allegorical preview of the Church. In the 7th century, Isidore of Seville (560-636) wrote in an encyclopedia of Biblical symbols that "Mary stands for the Church. For the Church is espoused to Christ, and as a virgin conceives us, and brings us to birth as a virgin" (*The Allegories*).

To understand this allegorical way of looking at Scripture properly, it is helpful to focus on the word *preview*. The word the Fathers use is 'type,' as in archetype. A 'type' is like a preview. For the Fathers, in their Biblical interpretation, every Old Testament 'type' has its fulfilment in a New Testament counterpart, and likewise, much in the New Testament is also replayed symbolically in Christian history. The commonest modern experience of such 'typological,' previewing readings of Scripture happens on Easter night, when we hear the reading about the Crossing of the Red Sea (from the book of Exodus), which is fulfilled in the *Resurrection* of Christ from the dead, and symbolised in our contemporary lives by the baptism of believers: the

Exodus is a 'type' of the Resurrection, and baptism is a sacramental or symbolic sharing in the Resurrection. Exodus is the forerunner or preview of the Resurrection, and baptism is its living recreation. So every 'type' has three lives, in the Old Testament, the New Testament, and in the life of the Church. When the Fathers, like Irenaeus and Augustine, claimed that Eve was the 'type' of Mary, the allegorical preview of Mary, they meant that Eve's meaning for humanity was completed or realised in Mary. Thus, they call *Mary* the "Mother of the living," because Eve is like a trailer for Mary, and Eve's allegorical significance is completely viewed, and lived, in Mary. Mary, in her turn, is, as Isidore says, summing up five centuries of earlier theology, the allegory of the Church.

Mary without sin

Mary epitomises the Church. This is at the heart of the meaning of the 'Immaculate Conception' of Mary, the teaching that, from the moment of her conception, Mary was without sin. When we speak of the allegorical or symbolic significance of a Biblical character or event, we are thinking of the meaning which God gives it and which is actualised in human history. Eve, the first human woman, was intended by God to live in Paradise, eternally sinless and at one with God. It is in this that she previews the sinlessness of Mary. The allegories or symbols in the Old Testament are not just buried deep inside the *words*, so that a very clever person could dig them out. The historical events of the New Covenant make those of the Old Testament symbolical: That is why we can only understand the Old Testament in the light of the New. In a sense, Eve only *becomes* a type or preview of Mary when paradasial innocence is regained, by Mary. Augustine wrote that, 'But already then, Mary was included in Eve; yet it was only when Mary came, that we knew who Eve was.' [*Sermon* 102].

The statement in Genesis 3, that a woman will crush the serpent's head, comes to life in the sinlessness of Mary, the defeat of the original sin of Adam and Eve in her. But not only in her, as an historical individual. In her immaculate conception, Mary is the archetype of the Church. She is what God intended for all humanity, for all "the living" of whom she is the "mother." This is why the Church teaches that Mary is the fulfilment of Eve: God's plan for humanity, begun in Eve, is completed in Mary – and therefore, in the Church. Saint Paul in his letters taught the first Christians that God intended them to be 'holy and unspotted' (*immaculati*) before Him (*Ep* 1:4; cf. *Col* 1:22). The Church of all Christians is to be *immaculate*. God has already made it so in Mary, and

Mary is not immaculate as a beautiful lady on a pedestal, but *in and on behalf of the Church*. As the grumpy saint Jerome wrote in the 5th century, 'All that we lost through the curse upon Eve is restored *to us* through the blessing upon Mary...for she is the immaculate one, untouched by sin". Mary's blessing belongs to us. Her sinlessness was not given to her by God as a private possession, but as a symbolic milestone on the way to the holiness which He wills to achieve by grace in all Christians. Hugo Rahner writes that the "word 'immaculate'...sums up the mystery of our own spiritual life. We are members of the Church, and in us the Church's mystery must be accomplished: it begins with Mary Immaculate, and we in our turn, by the power of the Holy Spirit, must once more become immaculate. In each of us the victory over the serpent must be achieved. Each of us must once more find entry to the paradise lost from which Mary was never excluded, entry to the eternal company of God, presented, as saint Jude says, 'spotless before the presence of His glory with exceeding joy."

Mary in the Church Fathers

One of the main sources of early Christian Mariology is Patristic and Mediaeval commentaries on the book of Revelation. It is a pity that these Biblical commentaries are not more widely known, because people often tune out from Bible readings in Church which are bizarre and puzzling, and those we hear on the Feast of the Assumption of Mary are just that. On this Feast, we usually hear a text from Revelation 12 such as this: "A great sign appeared in the sky, a woman clothed with the sun, with the moon under her feet, and on her head a crown of twelve stars. She was with child and wailed aloud in pain as she labored to give birth. Then another sign appeared in the sky; it was a huge red dragon, with seven heads and ten horns, and on its heads were seven diadems. Its tail swept away a third of the stars in the sky and hurled them down to the earth. Then the dragon stood before the woman about to give birth, to devour her child when she gave birth. She gave birth to a son, a male child, destined to rule all the nations with an iron rod. Her child was caught up to God and his throne... Then the dragon became angry with the woman and went off to wage war against the rest of her offspring, those who keep God's commandments and bear witness to Jesus" (*Rv* 12:1-5, 17). Patristic and Mediaeval theologians believed that the woman crowned with the stars is Mary, because Mary is represented here as both the God-bearer (*Theotokos*) and the 'Church bearer', the woman who gives birth to the Church. The "rest of her offspring" are Christians, against whom Satan is at war until the end of the world.

Jesus born in every Christian

At the very same time, the Woman in labour is understood to be the Church, that is, *every Christian*. The passage has more than one level of meaning: literally, it is about Mary, but symbolically, it is about the Church. Because the woman in childbirth is Mary, she simultaneously stands for the Church. But how can the *present day* Church be in labour with the Christ child, when he was born long ago in Bethlehem, and died and ascended to heaven, 'under Pontius Pilate' (that is, in around 33 AD)? Many of the Fathers of the Church interpreted this text as depicting the birth of Christ within our souls: for our rebirth in Christ is also his rebirth in us, his living in us. In the third century, Hippolytus wrote that "The Church never ceases to give birth to the Logos' [the Word]. 'And she brought forth a man-child who was to rule all nations' says the text: the perfect man that is Christ, the child of God, both God and man. And the Church brings forth this Christ when she teaches all nations" [*De Antichristo*, 61]. In a sermon on Revelation 12, Gennadius of Marseilles observed that, "The Church is ever in travail to bring forth the one Christ in His members".

The ultimate meaning of the Assumption, as expressed in the readings from Revelation for this Feast, is that God intends each of us to be a 'mother' to Christ, a God-bearer. This helps us to understand that Matthew 12:47-50, where Jesus sends his mother and brothers packing with the words that everyone who does his will is his mother and sister and brother, is not directed against his mother. Rather, He intends to *include* all believers within his mother, as the believing Church. Writing about Revelation in the 12th century, the French mystic Richard of Saint Victor observed that "The holy Church is striving with all her might to do the will of the Father, in order to become the mother of Christ. For the Church all-holy becomes Christ's mother, whenever she strives to do what is pleasing to the Father: she conceives Him in her womb through the power of grace in the faith, she gives Him birth through her holy desire, she has Him as her child through her good works."

Mary the 'sign'

Mary is the prophetic *sign* of the destiny intended for all believers, the life of divine grace. There is more to this than being a *picture* of perfection. We don't like to do or say certain things because we think they are 'bad luck signs' – signs that bring about bad 'luck'. Perhaps in calling Mary our "blessing" Jerome intended to say she is a good 'luck' sign – she *brings about* the blessing. The "great sign" spoken of by the book of Revelation is Mary in her mission of giving birth to both Christ, and the Church. Mary is not just the archetype of the Church, like the formula in God's mind for what the perfect Church will be like one day. Mary is the woman whose co-operation enables God to fulfil his will for humanity, that all be saved. That is why she is the symbol of the Church. As a real woman, she stands for the fact that the Church has a "personal form". "In theology," Joseph Ratzinger says, "it is not the person that is reducible to the thing, but the thing to the person"[15]: the Church does not come down to a thing, like an institution or corporation, but to a person.

Mary &
Christian faith

How our faith in God is like Mary's

Because the whole orientation of our secular culture is toward informality, we tend today to speak of 'Mary,' rather than, as was common in the quite recent past, 'the blessed Virgin Mary.' A whole theology is concentrated in those four words, and you may find that if you come to use them spontaneously, this theology has somehow entered your way of looking at things. To call Mary most blessed is to say she is the *luckiest* person who ever lived. For the life of the Triune God is one of *happiness*, and the more warmly a person shares in God's divine life, the happier or more *blessed* he or she is. The 'Hail Mary' repeats Elizabeth's address to Mary, 'blessed art thou among women,' and calls her 'full of grace.' God enables us to share in his divine, supernatural life by giving us something of himself. These gifts of the divine life are graces, touches of God.

God's grace makes the supernatural virtues of faith, hope and charity *dwell* in us. Thus, to call Mary 'full of grace,' or 'blessed,' is to say that faith, hope and love inhabit everything that she is and does.

The Annunciation

Consider the most widely illustrated scene of Mary's life. An angel appears to a Jewish girl, and tells her that she will bear the 'son' of Yahweh, the most high God (*Lk* 1:32). What sense could she make of this, within the monotheistic Jewish tradition? We know from the depiction of the disciples' stumbling efforts to understand, and from the utter rejection of Jesus' claims by many of his Jewish contemporaries, how near to impossible it was for a Jew to believe that God could have a *son*. The disciples and Jesus' other hearers were given aids to understanding, from Jesus' miracles and his teaching. When she heard the angel's request that she consent to God's plan, Mary had none of this. For her, it had to be a matter of putting her trust and faith in God's word. This faith in God, made possible by God's grace, was an act of committing herself into God's hands. There are many modes or ways of sharing in the divine life of grace. When Mary said, 'Let it be done to me according to your will,' she chose to share in the divine life in the mode of faith in God's will. As Benedict XVI put it in a sermon on the Assumption, "the words of Elizabeth that are completed in Mary's Magnificat" are 'Blessed is she who believed.' ... Mary is 'blessed' because she had become - totally, in body and soul, and forever - the dwelling of God.... 'Blessed is she who believed.' The first and fundamental act to becoming a dwelling of God, and to find happiness thereby, is to believe. Belief is faith, faith in God".[16]

The Simplicity of Mary

Having faith means holding as true something which one cannot fully *know* or *understand* to be true. Faith and understanding are different ways of knowing something, but they are not opposed. Luke tells us that Mary *pondered* these things in her heart (*Lk* 2:19; 2:51). An object of faith is a subject of wonder, of pondering without being able to compute. You know that, although familiarity by itself breeds contempt, familiarity combined with love breeds a sense of mystery. The closer you are to someone, the more mysterious they may seem. Because Mary had the greatest intimacy of all human beings with the Incarnate God, she knows more than any other how mysterious God is, how much God is a subject of faith rather than of mere understanding. The 'darkness' of Mary's faith is the darkness of proximity to the divine light. This isn't the self-willed blindness of one who keeps their eyes shut and refuses to think, but an open-eyed consent to living day by day from faith in God's providential care and wisdom. Mary's faith is not the ignorance which some people identify with bliss, but the grace filled, lucky, ability to ponder the wisdom of God.

It may be difficult to imagine how someone who was so miraculously singled out by God should really need *faith*. In Georges Bernanos' great novel, *The Diary of a Country Priest*, the Curé of Torcy describes Mary's sinlessness as entailing an *innocence* so complete that it includes ignorance *of her own importance*: "A little girl, the queen of the Angels! And she's *still* a little girl, remember", the old priest says. He goes on, "But you can't stop fools from reconstructing 'the drama of the incarnation,' as they call it! People...are too nervous to tell unbelievers that the one and only drama, the drama of dramas – since there is no other – was played without scenery, was never really staged. Think of it! The Word was made Flesh and not one of the journalists of those days even knew it was happening! ... And it's just the same with miracles. He performs no more than necessary. Miracles are the pictures – the pretty pictures in the book. But remember this, lad, Our Lady knew neither triumph nor miracle. Her Son preserved her from the least tip-touch of the savage wing of human glory. No one has ever lived, suffered, died in such simplicity, in such deep ignorance of her own dignity, a dignity crowning her above the angels. For she was *born* without sin – in what amazing isolation! A pool so clear, so pure, that even her own image – created only for the sacred joy of the Father – was not to be reflected. The Virgin was Innocence."[17]

Mary Mother of the Christian

When a candidate is presented for baptism, the priest asks him or her what they are asking for, and the response is 'faith.' When we are baptised, God gives us what we ask, the supernatural gift of faith. Baptism is a rebirth, from a life which is oriented to death into a new life oriented to eternity. The baptismal candidate is asked where the path of faith leads, and the answer is 'life everlasting.' Like evangelical Protestantism, Catholicism puts being 'born again' at the basis and beginning of Christian life. It is not just a further step, but a new beginning, into another, and different life. With this emphasis on new *birth*, it is natural that Catholics should think of Christian faith as born *from someone* – from the blessed Virgin. In the second century, Irenaeus put the belief of Catholics like this: "How is mankind to escape this birth into death, unless he were born again through faith, by that new birth from the Virgin, the sign of salvation that is God's wonderful and unmistakable gift?" Baptism is a birth 'through faith,' birth to a life in the mode of faith in God's promises. A baptised person is a believer, like Mary, one who ponders without being able to compute. The importance of saying that the life of faith follows on "new birth from the Virgin" is that *we* don't choose to have faith any more than we chose to be born. If Catholics spoke of being 'born again' without saying *from whom* they are born, it could sound like they had decided for themselves to enter on some course of self-improvement. But in fact, we don't click on 'faith' out of an array of potential life-styles. We don't select faith, and nor do we invent the contents of our faith. Like life itself, faith is a gift from God. That's why it's called a 'supernatural virtue', a quality no one can just 'naturally' have, without God's grace.

Mary and hope

Mary knows the meaning of a 'hopeless' situation

To call Mary 'blessed', or lucky, is a paradox, like Jesus describing his crucifixion as his moment of greatest glory. We naturally gloss over the hardness of the path which Mary took, when she said 'Yes', to the Angel and to God. In fact, Mary had as much reason as anyone has ever had to expect the worst. Although it is just fiction, Anne Rice's novel about the childhood of Jesus, *Christ the Lord: Out of Egypt*, makes a good stab at imagining what the life of a young Jewish woman who was known by her neighbours and kin to have engaged in a 'shotgun marriage' to an older man, may have been like. The gossiping about hanky-panky won't have disappeared at Jesus' birth. Mary figures in *Out of Egypt* as a tough, *lonely* woman. She lives alone with the incommunicable secret of the conception of the son of God. She could share what she knew with very few, with Joseph and Elizabeth, and no-one could entirely understand. This novelistic portrayal rings true with what we know of her history. When she set out on the way of faith, Mary also embarked upon an apparently hopeless role. For the circumstances and the people all seemed to be against her – the very nature of hopelessness. And when the 'secret' began to come out, with the start of Jesus' ministry, rather than leading to her immediate vindication, it leads to her being further vilified by her kin, and to Jesus himself expelling them all (*Mk* 3:31-35; it will be interesting to see what Anne Rice does with this in the later instalments of the novel).

The secret of Mary

Mary did not just 'have' a secret, but *was* a secret, unrewarded, invisible woman. What could Mary make of the paradox that the cross is the glorification of Christ, when she stood for nine hours to watch her son being crucified? The events are all so much larger than this one little woman. No one empathises, and she became the archetypal nobody, whom no one sees: "the synoptic Gospels do not even notice her among the devout women at the foot of the Cross. Several of them are named, but she is not. Perhaps she stands there, together with John, keeping herself to herself, distant from the others, lost in the crowd of Roman soldiers, of people who had come to gape and mock and the crowds of people streaming in and out of the city past the crosses on the day before the feast: some poor woman."[18]

In these situations, Mary was able to *hope* that God's plan was being accomplished in her life. According to Thomas Aquinas, the object of the supernatural virtue of *hope* is "a future good, difficult but *possible* to obtain."[19] We cannot *hope* for the impossible. You can no more *hope* that the sun will come up than you can really *hope* that it won't: for hope is different from both rational expectation and fantasy. Remember that Mariology "is the definitive Yes to creation... undergirding faith in creation": if she could really *hope*, and not just dream, her object was "possible to obtain", however tiny the possibility might seem in relation to overbearing circumstances. What made it possible for Mary to hope in her mission was just the 'secret' which she held in her heart. It was by recalling the *memory* of this 'secret' that she was able to hope. John Paul II pictures Mary as living from the "memories of Jesus, impressed upon her heart". These "memories were", he says, "always with her,...the 'rosary' she recited uninterruptedly throughout her life."[20]

Close to Christ and close to us

Lumen Gentium says that Mary "occupies a place in the Church which is highest after Christ and yet very close to us."[21] She is "very close" in that, for her as for us, holding on to her mission was at one time what Dr. Johnson called "the triumph of hope over experience"; she is the "highest after Christ" because hope won out. Mary never ceased to hope, even when all hope seemed lost, because her hope rested in memories which she turned over in her imagination and in her thoughts. These memories enabled her, not to dwell in the past, but to live out her mission in the present – the very meaning of hope. She could remember that the Angel had told her, "no word shall be impossible with God" (*Lk* 1:36).

Like Mary, each of us has a mission from God. Our mission is not primarily *doing* something, but being someone, the person which God wills to create in us. Luck is divine providence when you know and give thanks for its source. The Old Testament describes several barren women, like Sarah and Hannah, to whom God gave children. In Mary, God topped this line by giving a son to a virgin. Mary's Magnificat gives thanks for God's doing great things in 'no-hopers.' The Magnificat is the opposite of a hymn we used to sing on Old Girls day, in my all girls' school, "Let us now praise Famous Men." The Magnificat praises all that God has done for humble, poor and hungry folk. Mary spontaneously *remembers* because she sums up in herself the history of Israel, a history in which the underdogs have overcome, by having the simplicity to co-operate with God's grace.

People willingly take their burdens to Mary because they feel instinctively that she knows the meaning of an apparently hopeless situation. She learned through many sufferings that her mission is to be there for someone else. We share in the grace of constant hopefulness given to her by God, by remembering her, and thereby making the charge of the past actual in our own present day missions. The Magnificat expresses Mary's mission. Mary exemplifies that hope which gushes up 'from below,' from the apparently hopeless cause.

Mary and love
Mary - the Church as the Bride of Christ

The supernatural love of Mary and the Church for God is the love of a *bride* for her husband. In the Old Testament, Israel is spoken of by the prophets as God's often wayward bride. For instance, in Hosea, God tells Israel that he "will betroth you to myself for ever, betroth you with integrity and justice, with tenderness and love; I will betroth you to myself in faithfulness, and you will come to know Yahweh' (*Ho* 2:10-20; cf. *Jr* 31:3; *Is* 54:5-6, etc). Saint Paul was building on this when he identified the relation between God and the Church with that between a husband and a wife: "Husbands, love your wives just as Christ loved the church and gave himself for her" (taken from Ephesians 5:22-33; it's worthwhile reading the whole passage).

We become lovable when we are loved. Both in the Old Testament prophets and in Paul, the *love* between God and the bridal Church means a love in which God is the wooer, not the wooed. God makes the Church worthy of being a bride. As Michelle Schumacher says, "the love of the divine Bridegroom is always primary vis-à-vis his bride, the church... It is the sacrificial love of the divine Bridegroom - even unto death - that makes his bride *lovable*, that bestows upon her the dignity of having been chosen and beloved; and it is this love that invests her with the power...to love in return,... 'we love, because he first loved us' (1 *Jn* 4:19)."[22] The Church is God's *beloved*, and it is God, the ardent Lover, whose creative seeing and call makes her a lover in return.

Paul exhorted Christian husbands to "love your wives, as Christ also loved the Church and delivered himself up for it: that he might sanctify it, cleansing it by the laver of water in the word of life, that he might present it to himself, a glorious Church, not having spot or wrinkle or any such thing, but that it should be holy and without blemish [*sancta et immaculata*]' (*Ep* 5:25-27). Because Paul says the Church is immaculately beautiful, all Christian commentators, from surprisingly early on, about the 2nd century, to the end of the Middle Ages, interpreted the Old Testament's "Song of Songs" to be an allegory of the love between Christ and his Church (and we have no way of knowing that the ancient poem's original, literal meaning was not in fact allegorical; the very strangeness of the love Song counts in favour of this). Just as the beloved is called 'perfect' by the lover in the Song of Songs, so the Church is 'immaculate,' in Mary. And this immaculate perfection is God's gift to the Church, in Mary. As Augustine says, in words always cited by the mediaeval commentators on the Song of Songs, "Thus saith the Lord: my sister art thou by my blood, my love art thou by my coming, my dove art thou by my spirit, but my perfect one art thou by my word, which them to the full hast received from my mouth" [*Tract in John* 57:4].

The Church is Immaculate in Mary

Much of the Church does not look, and is not, immaculate or perfect: it is frequently complicit in, and silent about evils. In this present age, the Church is immaculate, perfect and perfectly lovable, only in Mary, who has been given by God the grace of being in full what all the redeemed will become at the end of time. Without the beauty of Mary, one could only envisage the Church as a rather large and unwieldly corporate organization. Without her human perfection to underlie their teaching mission, the hierarchy of the Church could not teach the truth, for truth is grounded in *perfect* love. Mary's responsive love for Christ, the Bridegroom, is the deepest love given to Him by humankind. As the *Catechism* says, "holiness is measured according to the 'great mystery' in which the Bride responds with the gift of love to the gift of the Bridegroom. Mary goes before us all in the holiness that is the Church's mystery as 'the bride without spot or wrinkle.'" Without Mary, the Church would have perfect testimony, for its teachings, the witness of Peter and the other apostles, but it would be cut off from the perfect sanctity without which evidence is fruitless. The *Catechism* teaches therefore that "the 'Marian' dimension of the Church precedes the 'Petrine'" or institutional.[23] Without the real personification of sinlessness in Mary, our priests could not carry out their role of performing the sacraments. Although that objective role does not require any specific priest to be sinless, it does require perfect sanctity at the *root* of the Church. This root is Mary, in her perfect, "spotless" love for God. The Church is not a teaching and sacramentalising machine, but a person, a bride.

Mary's Intercession

The Fathers of the Second Vatican Council described Mary's mission when they said that she "occupies a place in the Church which is highest after Christ and yet very close to us."[24] Mary's mission, the special vocation given her by God, was to be there for others. Her openness to others was exhibited when she replied to the Angel's request that she become the Mother of the 'son' of the Most High God, 'Let it be done to me according to your word.' A quite ordinary analogy can help us to understand what it means to be open for others. There are those who especially participate in the public life of the institutions in which they work, for instance, a head-mistress in a school, or the Dean in a University. These are 'public figures,' those who have chosen a public rather than a relatively private life. The rest of us may observe their rise to public office and power with some cynicism. But there is one admirable thing about public figures: with one appointment following another, they must always be on call, never in the working day given much space for private absorption in their own thoughts, always available. Mary is the supreme 'public figure,' one whose mission it is to be there for those who need her to be "close" to them. A successful public figure cannot be rigid; they have to be flexible. If one transposes the analogy of the public person into theological understanding, it is someone who is soul and body at the disposal of God and his Church. God has used his grace to mould every sort of temperament and personality, adventurous missionaries, scholars, and hospice workers. All of these are 'public' servants of the Church to some degree. In Mary, the fullness of grace consists in an availability to others so deep and integral that it is able to be the source of the Church. When we consider what she is, in full, we see how our little public missions within the Church are partial reflections of her total dedication *to being what the Church is for* – a gift of oneself to others. Being for others is part of what we do, as Christians; in Mary, it is what she *is* (it can become so in us).

Hans Urs von Balthasar has written some lines on this which are worth rereading several times over: "it is Christ, not Mary, who brought the Church into being by his Passion. All the same, she took part, as an intermediary, in this creation by the universality and unrestrictedness of her Fiat, which the Son is able to use as an infinitely plastic medium to bring forth from it new believers, those born again. Her presence with him at the Cross, her agreement to his abandonment of her to the Church in the midst of his dereliction on the Cross" (when he handed her to John, saying 'son, behold your mother' - *Jn* 19:26-27), "her eternal role as the woman in labour (*Rv* 12), show how fully her self-surrender is universalized to become the common source, the productive womb, of all Christian grace."[25]

Mary's Protection

When the Church Fathers and Mediaevals like Hippolytus, Augustine, Alcuin, Bede, and many others, read in Revelation of "a woman clothed with the sun, and the moon under her feet" they said that the woman, Mary or the Church, is the moon, and that Christ is the Sun (with no pun intended, for not even the Northumbrian Alcuin wrote in our modern English). We have said that Mary is quite different from an ancient, pre-historical fertility goddess, for the latter represents human needs whereas Mary is given to us by God. But we have also seen that Marian devotion reflects the fact that, as Thomas Aquinas said, "grace does not abolish nature, but fulfils it."[26] God's gift to us of Mary does not abolish our natural needs and yearnings, including those expressed on the ancient caves and in prehistorical art, but fulfils them. The Fathers of the Church were responding to very 'primitive' human perceptions when they linked the moon to the woman and mother. These perceptions are none the less true and universal for being ancient. The desire for protection and shelter goes deep in human nature.

The first and most obvious way in which we ask Mary for protection is that we ask her to pray for us. '*Pray for us*', we say, '*ora pro nobis*'. The second half of the 'Hail Mary' asks for her to 'pray for us sinners now and at the hour of our death' – the two occasions of greatest need! There are three references to human temporality in this request: 'now', 'at the hour' and 'death'. Mary is the eschatological 'woman' of the Book of Revelation. And the medium in which she works is human time. She carries out her public mission by attending to the 'times' which matter to ordinary human beings. An expert, like a doctor or a vet, can help us within the field of their expertise. Mary is a technician of ordinary *time*. Her expertise is in helping us through the *times* of our lives. For she assisted in the incarnation of God in human *history*.

That is one reason why Marian devotions have often been localised by reference to a chain of events in the life of Christ. Before the rosary achieved its current form, there were many such 'historical' or temporal meditations, focused on imagining the sliding temporal phases of her life with Christ. Here are some from a 14th century 'Ave Psalm Psalter':

> Help us, because of the glances
> that he often cast toward you
> as a child toward its mother.
> Whatever you wish, he does for your sake.

Help us, Lady, on account of the agony
that Christ suffered on death's journey,
when Pilate washed his hands
that we may find a just end.[27]

The stages of our lives, its great Acts and minor scenes,
are known by Mary from the inside. John Paul II
observed that "No one has ever devoted himself to the
contemplation of the face of Christ as faithfully as
Mary."[28] His humanity was archetypal, the humanity of
one and all. Because she knows her Son most faithfully,
she knows humanity most profoundly. That is why we
invoke her help in the temporal path of our lives.

In Roman times, the Stoic philosophy taught that a true
philosopher disregards his bodily and emotional needs.
He remains *the same* under duress and in any situation,
because his rational nature rises above mere
circumstance. Stoicism has revived many times since
antiquity, always with the implication that the better sort
of person is capable of 'standing on his own two feet.'
Those who are devoted to Mary may frequently be
courageous and bold, but they are not Stoics. They feel no
dishonour in knowing they need shelter and protection,
and in asking for it. They are not self-reliant. They believe
that their strength lies in their weakness. Like saint Paul,
they see themselves as "the very least of all the saints" (*Ep*
3:8). And in this, their model is Mary herself.

Strength in Vulnerability

There is one way in which the images of pre-Christian art differ in entirety from our Christian devotion to Mary: whereas, for instance, the Greek and Egyptian goddesses are unanimously *happy* and powerful figures, Mary is very often shown in deepest mourning, watching the Crucifixion, or holding the lifeless body of her Son. Many of the older sort of statues of Mary, the sort styled by the Baroque artists and their imitators, cast her with a sword in her heart, or even seven swords. *The Passion of the Christ* has reminded us of why the image of the *Mater Dolorosa*, the Suffering Mother was dearly treasured by generations of believers in need of *help*. Joseph Ratzinger believed that such piety captures the basic truth about Mary: "Mary's path includes the experience of rejection (*Mk* 3:31-35; *Jn* 2:4). When she is given away under the Cross (*Jn* 19:29), this experience becomes a participation in the rejection that Jesus himself had to endure on the Mount of Olives (*Mk* 14.34) and on the Cross (*Mk* 15:34). Only in this rejection can the new come to pass...Marian piety is thus necessarily a passion-centred piety."[29] We can sum up much that has been said in this pamphlet in the words 'strength through vulnerability.' Chesterton never put paradox to greater effect than when he makes Mary appear to help Alfred rout the Danes: "and seven swords were in her heart/but one was in her hand."[30] Mary is powerful *because* she has suffered.

The book of Proverbs asked 'Who shall find a valiant woman?' (*Pr* 31:10) and the Mediaeval Bernard of Clairvaux replied by identifying this proverbial woman with our Lady, "A Lady full of bravery... Was she not indeed valiant, this woman, Mary, whose love was stronger than death?" Mary is spontaneously recognised as a protectress, a *mulieris fortis*, or what the French call a *femme fort*, *because* she stands for the vulnerability of the 'woman in labour' (*Rv* 12). The Stoics and their modern day heirs would not dream of thinking that the more vulnerable we are, the stronger. That is because their ideal, model human being is the young, athletic man, not the pregnant woman. It is in her maternal character that Mary is our powerful intercessor.

'Behold thy Mother'

If you have seen *The Passion of the Christ*, you will have realised imaginatively that it is possible for someone to give instructions in the course of being crucified; it is not one long blur of pain or abandonment. Mary is our mother first and foremost because that is Christ's wish. John's Gospel records that, as he suffered on the cross, he told his mother, 'Woman, behold thy son,' and he then told John, the beloved disciple, 'Behold thy mother' (*Jn* 19:26-27). With these words "Mary is given as a Mother" to the Church and "the Church is entrusted as a mystical child to 'the woman.'"[31]

All *mothers* are somehow bonded with their children. They 'know' what is happening with them. I say 'all' advisedly, for I once heard the interesting tale that certain Russian scientists had found mother *rabbits* to react when their babies were drowned in another room. Maclin Horton wrote an interesting commentary on this psychic connection:

"Among the many little things that have...impressed upon me the fact that men and women really are different psychologically was a moment twenty or so years ago when one of our daughters was a baby. My wife was changing the baby's nappies or giving her a bath, talking idly, partly to me and partly to our daughter, about what a beautiful baby she was, enumerating her delightful qualities, counting the toes and fingers, and so forth, adding at the end "And she has a tiny little mole here, here, here, here, and here," putting her finger on the spot with each "here," which involved turning her over for the last two or three. I remember being more than a little surprised that she had memorized the precise location of every variance in the baby's skin—there was no hesitation or searching involved as she jumped from one to the next... It was just a natural result of the amount of attention she gave the baby, the same mechanism which had once enabled me to sing effortlessly from memory every verse of Bob Dylan's eleven-minute 'Desolation Row.' I don't really think I loved our daughter any less, but I certainly didn't have such details at my command, and I imagine this pattern holds for most mothers and fathers.

The Nature of Motherhood

There's a humorous list of male-female differences floating around the Internet, one of those emails that circulate for years on end and thus presumably say something that hits home to a lot of people. On the topic of children, the anonymous writer notes a mother's very thorough knowledge of her children in every physical and mental respect, then says that 'A man is vaguely aware that there are some short people living in the house.'... Concomitant with that level of attention is something more subtle. Some part of a mother somehow goes out into the members of her family, especially her children. I can imagine that if one had the right parapsychological gift one would be able to see a psychic strand connecting them, through which some sort of unconscious communication takes place, an operation which requires that a part of the mother's soul go out into these strands. She is never altogether compact in

61

herself; some part of her is always with those she loves and for whom she feels responsible. No doubt this can be true of women in other relationships, and is probably true of some men, but by and large it's a feminine thing, and most strongly a mother-child thing."[32]

Christ's wish that Mary be Mother to the Church is rooted in the realities, in the nature of motherhood. Mary represents the Church theologically because that is the meaning of her created, factual motherhood. Catholic folk wisdom has always grasped Mary's 'psychic connection' with each of her children. Christ's giving Mary this role is based in the character of maternity. We appeal for Mary's intercession knowing that her maternal soul is always already intertwined with ours.

Mary is not just the 'eternal feminine,' the abstract and timeless essence of motherhood. She is, historically, the mother of Jesus Christ, and he is, for eternity, her Son. It is because she is His mother, that Mary is able to intercede with Christ for our needs. This is the ancient wisdom of the Church, and it is common sense, if you think about it.

Further Reading

On the Rosary

Aid to the Church in Need has an excellent pamphlet explaining how to say the Rosary: available from ACN, 1 Times Square, Surrey, SM1 1LF.

Benedict Groeschel, *The Rosary: Chain of Hope*, Ignatius, 2003.

John D. Miller, *Beads and Prayers: The Rosary in History and Devotion*, London, Burns & Oates, 2002.

On the Theology of Marian Devotion

All of the Patristic quotations in this pamphlet are taken from: Hugo Rahner SJ, *Our Lady and the Church*, translated by Sebastian Bullough OP, Bethesda, Maryland: Zaccheus Press. This book is probably the best starting point for beginners in Mariology.

To understand the contemporary Dogmatic framework of Marology, you can read the *Dogmatic Constitution on the Church*, from Vatican II: *Lumen Gentium*: Chapter VIII, "The Blessed Virgin Mary, Mother of God in the Mystery of Christ and the Church."

Recent papal teachings on Mary are found in:

Paul VI, *Marialis Cultis*, 'For the Right Ordering and Development of Devotion to the Blessed Virgin Mary', 1974.

John Paul II, *Redemptoris Mater*, 'On the Blessed Virgin Mary in the life of the Pilgrim Church, 1987.

John Paul II: *Rosarium Virginis Mariae*, 'Apostolic Letter on the Most Holy Rosary', 2002.

It will also be very helpful to consult the *Catechism of the Catholic Church*, looking up 'Mary' in the Index.

Other accessible books include

Hans Urs von Balthasar, *Mary for Today*, Ignatius Press, 1987.

Joseph Ratzinger and Hans Urs von Balthasar, *Mary: The Church at its Source*, Ignatius, 1997.

Joseph Ratzinger, *Daughter Zion: Meditations on the Church's Marian Belief*, Ignatius, 1983

More difficult books which take a bit of theology to understand include

Hans Urs von Balthasar, *Explorations in Theology II: Spouse of the Word*, Ignatius Press, 1991.

Sarah Jane Boss, *Empress and Haidmaid: Nature and Gender in the Cult of the Virgin Mary*, Continuum, 2000.

Sarah Jane Boss, *Mary*, Continuum, 2005.

Sarah Jane Boss and Tina Beattie, *A Marian Resource Book*, Continuum, 2007.

Brian E. Daley, *On the Dormition of Mary: Early Patristic Homilies*, St. Vladimir's Seminary Press, 1998.

Stephen J. Shoemaker, *The Ancient Traditions of the Virgin Mary's Dormition and Assumption*, Oxford University Press, 2003.

Some Books of General Interest

Anne Rice, *Christ the Lord: Out of Egypt*, Knopf, 2005.

Randall Sullivan, *An Investigation of Holy Visions*, Little, Brown, 2004.

Notes

[1] John Paul II, *Rosarium Virginis Mariae*, "Apostolic Letter on the Most Holy Rosary," (2002), #29.

[2] Ibid., # 14.

[3] Taken from John D. Miller, *Beads and Prayers: The Rosary in History and Devotion*, London: Burns & Oates, 2002, p. 17.

[4] *Lumen Gentium*, Chapter 8, especially sections 57-62.

[5] Hans Urs Von Balthasar, *Mary For Today*, translated by Robert Nowell, San Francisco: Ignatius Press, 1987, pp. 44-45.

[6] Joseph Cardinal Ratzinger, *Mary: The Church at the Source*, translated by Adrian Walker, San Francisco: Ignatius Press, 2005, p. 46.

[7] Eamon Duffy, *Faith of our Fathers*, London: Continuum, 2005, pp. 54-56.

[8] Christopher Derrick, *Sex and Sacredness: A Catholic Homage to Venus*, San Francisco: Ignatius Press, 1982, p. 73.

[9] Bruce Springsteen, "The Rising," on *The Rising*, 2001.

[10] Cited in Hugo Rahner S.J., *Our Lady and the Church*, translated by Sebastian Bullough O.P., First published in English by Darton, Longman and Todd/ Pantheon Books, 1961, Reprinted by Zaccheus Press, Bethesda, Maryland, p. 92.

[11] Ibid., p. 125.

[12] Ratzinger, *Mary: The Church at the Source*, p. 31.

[13] *Lumen Gentium*, Chapter 8, section 56.

[14] Ibid., Chapter 8, sections 53 and 61.

[15] Ratzinger, *Mary: The Church at the Source*, p. 27.

[16] Benedict XVI, "Sermon on the Assumption," 2006.

[17] Georges Bernanos, *The Diary of a Country Priest*, first published in French 1936, translated by Pamela Morris, New York: Carroll & Graf, 1937, pp. 210-211.

[18] Von Balthasar, *Mary for Today*, p. 65.

[19] Thomas Aquinas, *Summa Theologiae* II-II, q. 17, a. 1.

[20] John Paul II, "Rosarium," # 11.

[21] *Lumen Gentium*, Chapter 8, section 54.

[22] Michele M. Schumacher, *Women in Christ: Toward a New Feminism*, Grand Rapids: William B. Eerdmans, 2004, p. 219.

[23] *Catechism of the Catholic Church,* No 773, citing in part from John Paul II's encyclical *Mulieris Dignitatis.*

[24] *Lumen Gentium,* Chapter 8, # 54.

[25] Hans Urs von Balthasar, *Explorations In Theology* II: *Spouse of the Word,* translated by A.V. Littledale, Alexander Dru and John Saward, San Francisco: Ignatius Press, 1991, pp. 165-166.

[26] Thomas Aquinas, *Summa Theologiae* I, q. 1, a. 8.

[27] Quoted in Miller, *Beads and Prayers,* p. 50.

[28] John Paul II, "Rosarium," # 10.

[29] Joseph Ratzinger, *Mary: The Church at its Source,* p. 35.

[30] Chesterton, *The Ballad of the White Horse.*

[31] Rayner, *Our Lady and the Church,* p. 58.

[32] Maclin Horton, "Mother's Day,"
on *http://www.lightondarkwater.com/blog/index.html*

Mary in the Liturgy

The Virgin Mary remained beside Jesus from the manger to the cross – but how does she stay next to Christ and his Church today?

Drawing on Church teaching and history, liturgical expert Professor David W. Fagerberg, shows how Mary is central to the life and worship of the Church. She is the example for every Christian in her love for God and accompanies us all on our journey towards Him.

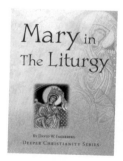

ISBN: 978 1 86082 791 4

CTS Code: SP36

The Litany of Loreto

This litany to the Blessed Virgin Mary was first used in the mid-16th century at the Italian shrine from which its name derives.

Now considered a classic text of Marian devotion, the Litany of Loreto is an opportunity to draw closer to Jesus' mother through seeing her as the greatest example of the Christian life.

This booklet, as well as containing the full text of the actual litany, also looks closely at the many titles used to describe Our Blessed Lady and how their meaning can help us to live as she did, ever open to God's plan.

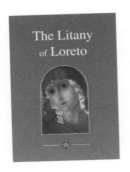

ISBN: 978 1 86082 796 9

CTS Code: D751

Marian Prayer Book

A collection of classic prayers to Mary, bound in imitation leather. This beautiful selection includes:

- All the most familiar and well-loved prayers
- Prayers from approved Marian Apparitions
- Marian prayers from the Eastern Church
- Marian Hymns

And many more, all contained in one attractively-bound volume.

The blue imitation leather cover adds beauty and durability to the book, which is a treasury of prayer to the Mother of God that will surely be a much-cherished companion.

ISBN: 978 1 86082 797 6

CTS Code: D752

Understanding the Rosary

The Rosary remains one of the most popular and enduring Marian devotions, especially since the addition of the Luminous Mysteries by Pope John Paul II. This booklet traces the origins of the Rosary prayer, explains the meaning, value and different ways of praying it, answers objections to it, and finally provides simple themes for meditation.

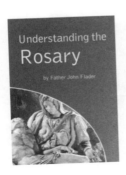

ISBN: 978 1 86082 627 6

CTS Code: D717

Companion to the Feasts of Mary

This handy Companion is designed to accompany the reader through the various feasts of the Virgin Mary as they occur during the year. Here you will find helpful historical background to the feasts, as well as Church teaching, scripture passages, spiritual writings and devotions. Where is Mary's place in the Christian's journey? Why does the Church celebrate these feasts? These questions are richly answered here in this true treasure chest finely collected and edited by Mr J.B. Midgley for the CTS.

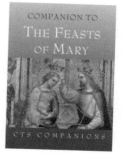

ISBN: 978 1 86082 055 7

CTS Code: Do656